I0801623

CHRISTOPHER ROUSE

DER GERETTETE ALBERICH

for percussion and orchestra

HENDON MUSIC
BOOSEY & HAWKES

Commissioned by the Cleveland Orchestra,
Christoph von Dohnányi, Music Director
with the generous assistance of the Kulas Foundation,
The Philadelphia Orchestra, Wolfgang Sawallisch, Music Director,
The Baltimore Symphony, David Zinman, Music Director,
and the London Symphony Orchestra,
for Evelyn Glennie

PROGRAM NOTE

One of Richard Wagner's most interesting decisions as creator of *Der Ring des Nibelungen* was to leave unclear the fate of Alberich, the villainous dwarf who has set in motion the inexorable machinery of destiny, leading in the end to apocalyptic cataclysm, which concludes *Götterdämmerung.* As is so often the case in Wagner's operas, Alberich is more than a cardboard villain in the Italian mode—as memorable as he is, a Scarpia, for example, is thoroughly and irredeemably maleficent. Alberich, on the other hand—like Frederic of Telramund, or Klingsor, or even Falfner—is not entirely unsympathetic; however cruel his actions, they are often the result of mistreatment at the hands of others. It is the Rhinemaidens' heartless mockery of him that leads Alberich to the theft of the gold, and it is Wotan's treachery that goads Alberich into placing his mighty curse on the ring he has fashioned from the gold (indeed, Wotan is something of a mirror image to Alberich, an essentially sympathetic character whose actions are often devious, even ignoble). Thus, it is possible with Alberich—and with many other Wagnerian villains—to recognize the inherent evil of his nature and deeds and yet still discern some measure of humanity in him and, in the process, to feel compassion for his plight.

As Alberich's whereabouts are unknown at the end of the *Ring*, it occurred to me that it might be engaging to return him to the stage, so to speak, so that he might wreak further havoc in what is quite literally the godless world in which Wagner has left us in the final pages of *Götterdämmerung.* The result was *Der gerettete Alberich*, whose title might best be translated as "Alberich Saved," itself a reference to Georg Kaiser's expressionist play *Der gerettete Alkibiades.* Rather than a concerto, *Der gerettete Alberich* is more of a fantasy for solo percussionist and orchestra on themes of Wagner, with the soloist taking on the "role" of Alberich. Much of the musical material in the work is derived from a number of motives associated with Alberich in the *Ring*, among them the motives for the curse, the power of gold, the renunciation of love, annihilation, the Nibelungs, and, of course, the Ring itself. Only Wagner's "Redemption through Love" motive stands beyond the ken of the other Alberich-related motives I have used, though I have rather maliciously distorted it to suit the purposes of my "hero."

Notwithstanding the discernible tripartite structure of *Der gerettete Alberich*, this work is somewhat looser architecturally than other scores of mine to which I have appended the title "concerto"—hence my decision to refer to it as a "fantasy." Having said all of the above, it would now be absurd of me to aver that this work is not programmatic; however, it is fair to say that it is not a narrative piece in the manner of, say, Strauss' *Don Quixote.* Beyond a brief passage in which Alberich serves a stint as a rock drummer (probably inspired, at least in part, by the wonderfully over-the-edge Wagner reincarnated scenes in Ken Russell's film, *Lisztomania*), I was not attempting to paint specific pictures in the score. However, the listener is free to provide whatever images he or she likes to the sonic goings-on.

Der gerettete Alberich was composed for percussionist Evelyn Glennie (to whom it is dedicated) and a commissioning consortium of the London Symphony Orchestra, the Cleveland Orchestra, the Philadelphia Orchestra, and the Baltimore Symphony Orchestra. The soloist's battery consists of four wood blocks, four log drums, four tom-toms, two bongos, two timbales, a snare drum, a steel drum, a marimba, two guiros, a pedal-operated bass drum, and a drum set. The orchestration calls for piccolo, two flutes, three oboes, three clarinets, three bassoons, six horns, three trumpets, three trombones, tuba, harp, timpani, percussion (three players), and strings. The percussion section makes use of chimes, antique cymbals, xylophone, castanets, tam-tam, bass drum, suspended cymbal, four tom-toms, anvil, and a thunder sheet.

Completed on June 7, 1997, *Der gerettete Alberich* lasts approximately 22 minutes in performance.

— Christopher Rouse

INSTRUMENTATION

Piccolo
2 Flutes
3 Oboes
3 Bb Clarinets
3 Bassoons

6 F Horns
3 C Trumpets
3 Trombones
Tuba

Harp
Timpani
Percussion (3 players)
- Antique cymbals
- Xylophone
- Chimes
- Suspended Cymbal
- Tamtam
- Anvil
- Thunder sheet
- 4 Tom-toms
- Bass Drum (kick drum)
- Tambourine
- Castanets
- Cowbell
- Large rachet

Strings

* Solo Percussion:

Station 1 (Center)
- 4 Wood Blocks
- 4 Log Drums
- 4 Tom-toms
- 2 Timales
- 2 Bongos
- 2 Quiros
- Snare Drum
- Pedal operated Bass Drum (kick drum)

Station 2 (Stage Left)
- Marimba (Standard Size)
- Two-Octave Chromatic Steel Drum

Station 3 (Stage Right)
- Drum Set consisting of:
- Snare Drum
- 3 Tom-toms
- 2 Suspended Cymbals
- Chinese Cymbal
- Bass Drum (pedal operated)
- Hi-Hat

Percussion Mallet Symbols

Symbol	Mallet	Symbol	Mallet	Symbol	Mallet
—SF	soft felt stick	—SR	soft rubber mallet		tamtam beater
—MF	medium felt stick	—MR	medium rubber mallet		gourd scraper
—HF	hard felt stick	—HR	hard rubber mallet		chime mallet
—SY	soft yarn mallet	—W	wood stick	—SD	snare drum stick
—MY	medium yarn mallet		hammer		bass drum beater
—HY	hard yarn mallet	—B	brass mallet		

Score is in C
Duration: *ca.* 22 minutes

* The solo percussionist plays from three stations placed close together (but still spatially separate) at the front of the stage. Though most of the soloists instruments are also to be found in the setup of station 1, it is preferable that, for visual reasons as well as practical ones, this drum set be a separate entity from the instruments in station 1.

—Christopher Rouse

to Evelyn Glennie

Der gerettete Alberich

Christopher Rouse
(1997)

First print 2021

Picc.
Fl. 1 2
Ob. 1 2
3
Cl. 1 2
3
Bsn. 1 2
3
Hn. 1 3
5 2
4 6
Tpt. 1 2
3
Tbn. 1 2
3 Tuba
Hp.
8va
Timp.
Perc. 1 2 3
Solo Perc.
Vn. I
non cresc.
Vn. II
non cresc.
div. a3
Va.
Vc.
unis.
Cb.
6 soli
niente
p
mf
ff
pp

1
senza misura
♩. = ♩ (♩ = 44)
Picc.
Fl.
Ob.
Cl.
Bsn.
Hn.
Tpt.
Tbn.
Tuba
Hp.
Timp.
gliss.
Perc.
Guiro 2 (very large)
like breathing
sim.
Guiro 1 (medium)
Solo Perc.
senza misura
♩. = ♩ (♩ = 44)
Vn. I
Vn. II
Va.
Vc.
6 Soli
gliss.
Cb.

accel. al ♩ = 66
accel. al ♩ = 92
accel. al ♩ = 132
accel. al ♩ = 152
Picc.
Fl. 1 2
Ob. 1 2 3
Cl. 1 2 3
Bsn. 1 2 3
Hn. 1 3 5 2 4 6
Tpt. 1 2 3
Tbn. 1 2 3
Tuba
Hp.
Timp.
gliss.
mp p
Perc. 1 2 3
Solo Perc.
mp pp f mf mp
mp mf mp
f pp f pp f
p ff
Vn. I
Vn. II
Va.
Vc.
Cb.
gliss.
mf p
gliss.
mf p

2
Presto, ♩ = 152
Picc.
Fl.
Ob.
Cl.
Bsn.
Hn.
1. con sord. (straight)
Tpt.
Tbn.
Tuba
Hp.
l.v.
G♮
E → G
Timp.
Perc.
Solo Perc.
Presto, ♩ = 152
Vn. I
Vn. II
(unis.)
Va.
(unis.)
Vc.
6 soli, div. (arco)
div. a2 (arco)
Cb.
pizz. gli altri
ff sub.

Picc.
Fl. 1 2
Ob. 1 2 3
Cl. 1 2 3
Bsn. 1 2 3
2.
mf
Hn. 1 3 5 2 4 6
Tpt. 1 2 3
Tbn. 1 2 3
Tuba
Hp.
Timp.
Perc. 1 2 3
Solo Perc.
Vn. I
Vn. II
Va.
Vc.
Cb.

3
Picc.
Fl.
Ob.
Cl.
Bsn.
Hn.
Tpt.
Tbn.
Tuba
Hp.
Timp.
Perc.
Solo Perc.
Vn. I
Vn. II
Va.
Vc.
Cb.
a2
2.

Picc.
Fl.
Ob.
Cl.
Bsn.
Hn.
Tpt.
Tbn.
Tuba
Hp.
Timp.
Perc.
Solo Perc.
Vn. I
Vn. II
Va.
Vc.
Cb.
unis.

4
Picc.
Fl.
Ob.
Cl.
Bsn.
Hn.
1. senza sord.
Tpt.
Tbn.
Tuba
Hp.
Timp.
Perc.
Wood Blocks
Solo Perc.
Bass Drum
(with foot pedal)
Vn. I
Vn. II
Va.
Vc.
Cb.

5
Picc.
Fl. 1 2
Ob. 1 2 3
Cl. 1 2 3
Bsn. 1 2 3
Hn. 1 3 5 2 4 6
Tpt. 1 2 3
Tbn. 1 2 3 Tuba
Hp.
Timp.
Perc. 1 2 3
Solo Perc.
Wood Block 4
Vn. I
Vn. II
Va.
Vc.
Cb.

Picc.
Fl.
Ob.
Cl.
Bsn.
Hn.
Tpt.
Tbn.
Tuba
Hp.
Timp.
Perc.
Solo Perc.
Vn. I
Vn. II
Va.
Vc.
Cb.

6
Picc.
Fl. 1 2
Ob. 1 2 3
Cl. 1 2 3
Bsn. 1 2 3
Hn. 1 3 5 2 4 6
Tpt. 1 2 3
Tbn. 1 2 3
Tuba
Hp.
Timp.
G → A♭
Perc. 1 2 3
Solo Perc.
Timbales
SD
Bongos
Vn. I
Vn. II
Va.
Vc.
Cb.

Picc.
Fl. 1 2
Ob. 1 2 3
Cl. 1 2 3
mf
mp
Bsn. 1 2 3
Hn. 1 3 5 2 4 6
Tpt. 1 2 3
Tbn. 1 2 3
Tuba
Hp.
Timp.
Perc. 1 2 3
Solo Perc.
mp mf
* press (do not roll)
Vn. I
Vn. II
Va.
Vc.
Cb.

7
Picc.
Fl.
Ob.
Cl.
Bsn.
Hn.
Tpt.
Tbn.
Tuba
Hp.
Timp.
Perc.
Solo Perc.
Rim Shot
Vn. I
Vn. II
Va.
Vc.
Cb.
pizz.

Picc.
Fl. 1 2
Ob. 1 2 3
Cl. 1 2 3
Bsn. 1 2 3
Hn. 1 3 5 2 4 6
Tpt. 1 2 3
Tbn. 1 2 3
Tuba
Hp.
Timp.
Perc. 1 2 3
Solo Perc.
Vn. I
Vn. II
Va.
Vc.
Cb.
tr
p
ff
f
sfpp
mf

Picc.
Fl.
Ob.
Cl.
Bsn.
Hn.
Tpt.
Tbn.
Tuba
Hp.
Timp.
Perc.
Solo Perc.
Vn. I
Vn. II
Va.
Vc.
Cb.
HF
gliss.
div.
8va
arco
1.

8
Picc.
Fl.
Ob.
Cl.
Bsn.
Hn.
Tpt.
Tbn.
Tuba
Hp.
l.v.
A♯
F♯
B♮
Timp.
Perc.
Solo Perc.
Vn. I
Vn. II
Va.
Vc.
Cb.
unis., pizz.
arco
unis.
pizz.
8va

Picc.
Fl. 1 2
8va
1.
mf
mp
Ob. 1 2
3
mf
f
Cl. 1 2
3
Bsn. 1 2
3
Hn. 1 3
5 2
4 6
Tpt. 1 2
3
Tbn. 1 2
3 Tuba
Hp.
Timp.
Perc. 1
2
3
Solo Perc.
mf
p
mp
mfs
tr
p
Vn. I
Vn. II
Va.
Vc.
Cb.
arco
mf
f

9
Picc.
Fl.
Ob.
Cl.
Bsn.
Hn.
Tpt.
Tbn.
Tuba
Hp.
Timp.
Perc.
Solo Perc.
Timbales
SD -butt
Bongos
Vn. I
Vn. II
Va.
pizz., div.
Vc.
arco
Cb.
arco

Picc.
Fl.
Ob.
Cl.
Bsn.
Hn.
Tpt.
Tbn.
Tuba
Hp.
Timp.
Perc.
Wood Blocks
Solo Perc.
Vn. I
Vn. II
Va.
Vc.
Cb.

10
Picc.
Fl. 1 2
Ob. 1 2 3
Cl. 1 2 3
Bsn. 1 2 3
Hn. 1 3 5 2 4 6
Tpt. 1 2 3
Tbn. 1 2 3
Tuba
Hp.
Timp.
Perc. 1 2 3
Solo Perc.
Wood Blocks
4.
Vn. I
Vn. II
div. a3
Va.
Vc.
Cb.

Picc.
Fl. 1 2
Ob. 1 2
3
Cl. 1 2
3
Bsn. 1 2
3
a2
Hn. 1 3
5 2
4 6
Tpt. 1 2
3
Tbn. 1 2
3 Tuba
Hp.
Timp.
Perc. 1
2
3
Solo Perc.
Vn. I
Vn. II
Va.
Vc.
Cb.

11
Picc.
Fl. 1 2
Ob. 1 2
3
Cl. 1 2
3
Bsn. 1 2
3
Hn. 1 3
5 2
4 6
Tpt. 1 2
3
Tbn. 1 2
3 Tuba
3.
Hp.
Timp.
MF
A♭ → F
D♭ → B
Perc. 1
2
3
Solo Perc.
HR
mf sub.
Bass Drum
Vn. I
Vn. II
Va.
div., arco
unis.
Vc.
Cb.

Picc.
Fl.
Ob.
Cl.
Bsn.
con sord.
2. con sord.
4. con sord.
con sord. (straight)
con sord. (straight)
1. con sord. (straight)
Hn.
Tpt.
Tbn.
Tuba
Hp.
Timp.
Perc.
Solo Perc.
Vn. I
Vn. II
Va.
Vc.
Cb.

Picc.
Fl. 1 2
Ob. 1 2
3
Cl. 1 2
3
Bsn. 1 2
3
Hn. 1 3
5 2
4 6
Tpt. 1 2
3
Tbn. 1 2
3 Tuba
Hp.
Timp.
Perc. 1
2
3
Solo Perc.
Vn. I
Vn. II
Va.
Vc.
Cb.
mp
p
mf
f
div.
gliss.

12
vuota
Picc.
Fl.
Ob.
Cl.
Bsn.
Hn.
Tpt.
Tbn.
Tuba
Hp.
l.v.
Timp.
Perc.
Solo Perc.
poco sf sempre
Vn. I
Vn. II
Va.
Vc.
Cb.
vuota

vuota
Picc.
Fl.
Ob.
Cl.
Bsn.
Hn.
con sord.
con sord.
Tpt.
Tbn.
Tuba
Hp.
A♮
C♮
harp harmonics sound one octave higher than written
B♮ G♮
Timp.
Perc.
Solo Perc.
vuota
Vn. I
Vn. II
Va.
div.
pizz.
Vc.
Cb.

13
Picc.
Fl.
Ob.
Cl.
Bsn.
Hn.
(con sord.)
Tpt.
Tbn.
Tuba
Hp.
Timp.
Perc.
Tam-Tam
l.v.
Bass Drum
Solo Perc.
Log Drums
Tomtoms
MY
Vn. I
Vn. II
Va.
unis.
arco
Vc.
Cb.

Picc.
Fl. 1 2
Ob. 1 2 3
Cl. 1 2 3
Bsn. 1 2 3
Hn. 1 3 5 2 4 6
Tpt. 1 2 3
mf
mp
Tbn. 1 2
3 Tuba
Hp.
Timp.
Perc. 1 2 3
Solo Perc.
8va
Vn. I
pppp
mf
pppp
Vn. II
Va.
Vc.
Cb.

14
Picc.
Fl. 1 2
Ob. 1 2 3
Cl. 1 2 3
Bsn. 1 2 3
Hn. 1 3 5 2 4 6
Tpt. 1 2 3
Tbn. 1 2 3
Tuba
Hp.
Timp.
Perc. 1 2 3
Solo Perc.
Vn. I
div.
pppp
Vn. II
div.
pppp
Va.
pppp
Vc.
Cb.

Picc.
Fl.
Ob.
Cl.
Bsn.
Hn.
Tpt.
Tbn.
Tuba
Hp.
Timp.
Perc.
Solo Perc.
Vn. I
Vn. II
Va.
Vc.
Cb.

Picc.
Fl. 1 2
Ob. 1 2 3
Cl. 1 2 3
Bsn. 1 2 3
Hn. 1 3 5 2 4 6
Tpt. 1 2 3
Tbn. 1 2 3
Tuba
Hp.
Timp.
Perc. 1 2 3
Solo Perc.
Vn. I
Vn. II
Va.
Vc.
Cb.
senza sord.
1. senza sord.
unis.
F → E♭ B → C A♭ → E♭
Bongos
Tom-toms

15
♪. = ♩ (♩ = 202.6)
Picc.
Fl. 1 2
Ob. 1 2 3
Cl. 1 2 3
Bsn. 1 2 3
Hn. 1 3 5 2 4 6
Tpt. 1 2 3
Tbn. 1 2 3
Tuba
Hp.
C♯ F♯
C♮ E♭ F♭
Timp.
Perc. 1 2 3
Solo Perc.
Timbales
Tom-toms
(Bass Drum)
Vn. I
Vn. II
Va.
Vc.
Cb.

Picc.
Fl.
Ob.
Cl.
Bsn.
Hn.
Tpt.
Tbn.
Tuba
Hp.
Timp.
Perc.
Snare Drum
snares off
SD
Solo
Perc.
Vn. I
Vn. II
Va.
Vc.
Cb.

16
Picc.
Fl.
Ob.
Cl.
Bsn.
Hn.
Tpt.
Tbn.
Tuba
Hp.
Timp.
Perc.
Solo Perc.
Vn. I
Vn. II
Va.
Vc.
Cb.

Picc.
Fl.
Ob.
Cl.
Bsn.
Hn.
Tpt.
Tbn.
Tuba
Hp.
Timp.
Perc.
Solo Perc.
press, do not roll
Vn. I
Vn. II
Va.
Vc.
Cb.

17
Picc.
Fl.
Ob.
Cl.
Bsn.
Hn.
Tpt.
Tbn.
Tuba
Hp.
Timp.
Perc.
Solo Perc.
r.s.
X - on hoop
Vn. I
Vn. II
Va.
Vc.
Cb.

Picc.
Fl.
Ob.
Cl.
Bsn.
Hn.
Tpt.
Tbn.
Tuba
Hp.
Timp.
Perc.
Solo Perc.
Vn. I
Vn. II
Va.
Vc.
Cb.

18
Picc.
Fl. 1 2
Ob. 1 2 3
Cl. 1 2 3
Bsn. 1 2 3
Hn. 1 3 5 2 4 6
a2
ff
Tpt. 1 2 3
senza sord.
Tbn. 1 2
3 Tuba
Hp.
Timp.
Chimes
let all notes ring
Perc. 1 2 3
Solo Perc.
snares on
(ff)
8va
Vn. I
Vn. II
Va.
Vc.
Cb.
fff

Picc.
Fl.
Ob.
Cl.
Bsn.
Hn.
Tpt.
Tbn.
Tuba
Hp.
Timp.
Perc.
Solo Perc.
Vn. I
Vn. II
Va.
Vc.
Cb.
a2
ff
p
MF
(ff)
8va

19
Picc.
Fl.
Ob.
Cl.
Bsn.
Hn.
Tpt.
Tbn.
Tuba
Hp.
Timp.
Perc.
Solo Perc.
stick tip
center of drumstick
l.v.
gliss.
Vn. I
Vn. II
Va.
Vc.
Cb.

Picc.
Fl.
(1.)
Ob.
Cl.
1.
Bsn.
Hn.
4.
Tpt.
Tbn.
Tuba
Hp.
Timp.
l.v.
Perc.
Solo Perc.
tip
(tip of drumstick)
piu p
Vn. I
gliss.
II
Vn. II
(IV)
Va.
IV
Vc.
Cb.
III

20
Picc.
Fl. 1 2
Ob. 1 2 3
Cl. 1 2 3
(1.)
Bsn. 1 2 3
Hn. 1 3 5 2 4 6
Tpt. 1 2 3
Tbn. 1 2 3
Tuba
ppp
Hp.
Timp.
pp
low E♭ → F
high E♭ → A♭
Perc. 1 2 3
Solo Perc.
center
tip
snares off
p
Vn. I
Vn. II
Va.
Vc.
Cb.
gliss.
pp
ppp

vuota
Picc.
Fl. 1 2
Ob. 1 2 3
Cl. 1 2 3
Bsn. 1 2 3
Hn. 1 3 5 2 4 6
Tpt. 1 2 3
Tbn. 1 2 3
Tuba
Hp.
Timp.
Perc. 1 2 3
Solo Perc.
edge (of head)
mp
p
normale
Bass Drum
3
più p
vuota
Vn. I
Vn. II
Va.
Vc.
Cb.

21
Meno mosso, ma presto ♩ = 152
Picc.
Fl.
Ob.
Cl.
1.
2. simile (come sopra)
simile (come sopra)
Bsn.
mp
Hn.
Tpt.
Tbn.
Tuba
Hp.
Timp.
Perc.
Solo Perc.
Meno mosso, ma presto ♩ = 152
Vn. I
Vn. II
Va.
Vc.
p
mp
div. a2
Cb.

Picc.
Fl. 1 2
Ob. 1 2
3
Cl. 1 2
3
Bsn. 1 2
3
Hn. 1 3
5 2
4 6
Tpt. 1 2
3
Tbn. 1 2
3 Tuba
Hp.
Timp.
Perc. 1
2
3
Solo Perc.
Vn. I
Vn. II
Va.
Vc.
Cb.
(2.)
a2
ff
1.
mf
molto f
unis.

Picc.
Fl. 1 2
Ob. 1 2
Ob. 3
Cl. 1 2
Cl. 3
(1.)
Bsn. 1 2
Bsn. 3
Hn. 1 3
Hn. 5 2
Hn. 4 6
1.
Tpt. 1 2
Tpt. 3
Tbn. 1 2
3 Tuba
Hp.
Timp.
Perc. 1
Perc. 2
Perc. 3
Solo Perc.
Vn. I
Vn. II
Va.
Vc.
p sub. ff
Cb.
p sub. ff

22
Picc.
Fl. 1 2
Ob. 1 2
Ob. 3
Cl. 1 2
Cl. 3
Bsn. 1 2
Bsn. 3
Hn. 1 3
Hn. 5 2
Hn. 4 6
Tpt. 1 2
Tpt. 3
Tbn. 1 2
Tbn. 3
Tuba
Hp.
Timp.
C → A
Perc. 1
Perc. 2
Perc. 3
Solo Perc.
Vn. I
Vn. II
Va.
Vc.
Cb.
8va
a2
poco f

Picc.
Fl.
Ob.
Cl.
Bsn.
Hn.
Tpt.
Tbn.
Tuba
Hp.
Timp.
Perc.
Solo Perc.
Vn. I
Vn. II
Va.
Vc.
Cb.
a2
(ff)
ff
f
mf
1.

23
Picc.
Fl.
Ob.
Cl.
Bsn.
Hn.
Tpt.
Tbn.
Tuba
Hp.
Timp.
Perc.
Solo Perc.
Vn. I
Vn. II
Va.
Vc.
Cb.
Wood Blocks
Bongos
Timbales
Log Drums
Tomtoms
Bass Drum
MR
poco sf sempre
pizz.

Picc.
Fl. 1 2
Ob. 1 2 3
Cl. 1 2 3
Bsn. 1 2 3
Hn. 1 3 5 2 4 6
Tpt. 1 2 3
Tbn. 1 2 3
Tuba
Hp.
Timp.
Perc. 1 2 3
Solo Perc.
Vn. I
Vn. II
Va.
Vc.
Cb.
mf
mp
f

24
Picc.
Fl.
Ob.
Cl.
Bsn.
Hn.
Tpt.
Tbn.
Tuba
Hp.
l.v.
F♯
D♭
Timp.
Perc.
Solo Perc.
Vn. I
Vn. II
Va.
Vc.
Cb.

Picc.
Fl.
Ob.
Cl.
Bsn.
Hn.
Tpt.
Tbn.
Tuba
Hp.
Timp.
Perc.
Solo Perc.
Vn. I
Vn. II
Va.
Vc.
Cb.
F♭
G♭ D♮
F♮
C♯ A♯
sempre

25
Picc.
Fl. 1 2
Ob. 1 2 3
solo
p
mp
mf
f
Cl. 1 2 3
Bsn. 1 2 3
Hn. 1 3 5 2 4 6
Tpt. 1 2 3
Tbn. 1 2 3
Tuba
Hp.
F♭ G♮ C♮ F♮
l.v.
Timp.
Perc. 1 2 3
Solo Perc.
mf
(mf)
Vn. I
Vn. II
Va.
Vc.
Cb.

Picc.
Fl.
Ob.
Cl.
Bsn.
Hn.
Tpt.
Tbn.
Tuba
poco f
8va
Hp.
A♭
D♯ G♮
E♮ A♮
A♭
l.v.
Timp.
Perc.
Wood Blocks
Solo Perc.
arco
Vn. I
Vn. II
Va.
Vc.
Cb.
div.

26
Picc.
Fl. 1 2
Ob. 1 2
Ob. 3
Cl. 1 2
Cl. 3
Bsn. 1 2
Bsn. 3
Hn. 1 3
Hn. 5 2
Hn. 4 6
Tpt. 1 2
Tpt. 3
Tbn. 1 2
3 Tuba
Hp.
Timp.
Perc. 1
Perc. 2
Perc. 3
Solo Perc.
Vn. I
Vn. II
Va.
Vc.
Cb.

Picc.
Fl.
Ob.
Cl.
Bsn.
Hn.
Tpt.
Tbn.
Tuba
Hp.
Timp.
Perc.
Solo Perc.
Wood Block 4
Bass Drum
Vn. I
Vn. II
Va.
Vc.
Cb.

27
Picc.
Fl.
Ob.
Cl.
Bsn.
Hn.
Tpt.
Tbn.
Tuba
Hp.
Timp.
Perc.
Solo Perc.
Vn. I
Vn. II
Va.
Vc.
Cb.
1.
MF
A → B
Bass Drum

Picc.
Fl.
Ob.
Cl.
Bsn.
Hn.
Tpt.
1. con sord. (straight)
Tbn.
Tuba
Hp.
l.v.
Timp.
Perc.
Solo Perc.
Timbales
Bongo 1
Bongo 2
Vn. I
Vn. II
Va.
Vc.
Cb.
pizz.
arco

Picc.
Fl. 1 2
Ob. 1 2 3
Cl. 1 2 3
Bsn. 1 2 3
Hn. 1 3 5 2 4 6
Tpt. 1 2 3
Tbn. 1 2 3
Tuba
Hp.
Timp.
Perc. 1 2 3
Solo Perc.
Vn. I
Vn. II
Va.
Vc.
Cb.
arco
mf
f
mp
p
mfs
tr

Picc.
Fl.
Ob.
Cl.
Bsn.
Hn.
Tpt.
Tbn.
Tuba
Hp.
Timp.
Perc.
Solo Perc.
Vn. I
Vn. II
Va.
Vc.
Cb.
(1.)
a2
Bass Drum
arco
pizz.

28
Picc.
Fl.
Ob.
Cl.
Bsn.
Hn.
Tpt.
Tbn.
Tuba
pp
p possible
Hp.
Timp.
SF
Perc.
Solo Perc.
Log Drums
SY
Tom-toms
Vn. I
Vn. II
Va.
Vc.
Cb.
arco
mp

Picc.
Fl. 1 2
Ob. 1 2 3
Cl. 1 2 3
Bsn. 1 2 3
Hn. 1 3 5 2 4 6
Tpt. 1 2 3
Tbn. 1 2 3
Tuba
Hp.
Timp.
Perc. 1 2 3
Solo Perc.
Vn. I
Vn. II
Va.
Vc.
Cb.
arco
pppp
mf
pppp

29
Picc.
Fl. 1 2
Ob. 1 2 3
Cl. 1 2 3
Bsn. 1 2 3
Hn. 1 3 5 2 4 6
pp
pp
Tpt. 1 2 3
Tbn. 1 2 3
Tuba
Hp.
Timp.
Perc. 1 2 3
Solo Perc.
div.
pppp
Vn. I
div.
pppp
Vn. II
pppp
Va.
Vc.
Cb.

Picc.
Fl. 1 2
Ob. 1 2 3
Cl. 1 2 3
Bsn. 1 2 3
Hn. 1 3 5 2 4 6
Tpt. 1 2 3
Tbn. 1 2
Tuba 3
Hp.
Timp.
Perc. 1 2 3
Solo Perc.
Vn. I
Vn. II
Va.
Vc.
Cb.
3.
pp
p
più f
mp
mf
pppp

30
Picc.
Fl. 1 2
Ob. 1 2 3
Cl. 1 2 3
Bsn. 1 2 3
Hn. 1 3 5 2 4 6
Tpt. 1 2 3
Tbn. 1 2 3
Tuba
Hp.
Timp.
Perc. 1 2 3
Solo Perc.
Vn. I
Vn. II
Va.
Vc.
Cb.
p possible
B → B♭
D → C♯
A♭ → F
Bass Drum
div.
unis.

vuota
Picc.
Fl.
Ob.
Cl.
Bsn.
Hn.
Tpt.
Tbn.
Tuba
Hp.
l.v.
Timp.
Perc.
Solo
Perc.
unis.
vuota
Vn. I
Vn. II
Va.
Vc.
Cb.

vuota
Picc.
Fl.
Ob.
Cl.
Bsn.
Hn.
Tpt.
Tbn.
Tuba
Hp.
l.v.
E♮
G♮
Timp.
Perc.
Solo Perc.
Bongo 1 with fingers
Timbale 1
Timbales
Bongo 2
Tom-toms
vuota
Vn. I
Vn. II
Va.
Vc.
Cb.
div.
gliss.

31
Molto adagio (subito) (♩ = 44)
Picc.
Fl. 1 2
Ob. 1 2 3
Cl. 1 2 3
Bsn. 1 2 3
Hn. 1 3 5 2 4 6
Tpt. 1 2 3
Tbn. 1 2 3
Tuba
Hp.
Timp.
Perc. 1 2 3
Guiros
1. 2.
like a sigh
to Marimba
Solo Perc.
Molto adagio (subito) (♩ = 44)
Vn. I
Vn. II
div. a3
pp dolce
div.
pp dolce
Va.
Vc.
Cb.

32
accel. al
♩ = 58
Picc.
Fl.
Ob.
Cl.
Bsn.
Hn.
Tpt.
Tbn.
Tuba
Hp.
Timp.
Perc.
Solo Perc.
Marimba
HY
pppp
mf
pppp
(avoid playing tremolo on this instrument unless specifically notated)
accel. al
♩ = 58
Vn. I
Vn. II
Va.
Vc.
Cb.

Picc.
Fl. 1 2
Ob. 1 2 3
Cl. 1 2 3
Bsn. 1 2 3
Hn. 1 3 5 2 4 6
Tpt. 1 2 3
Tbn. 1 2 3
Tuba
Hp.
Timp.
Perc. 1 2 3
Solo Perc.
(Mar.)
pppp
mf
pppp
pp
p
mp
Vn. I
Vn. II
Va.
Vc.
Cb.

33
Picc.
Fl.
Ob.
Cl.
Bsn.
Hn.
Tpt.
Tbn.
Tuba
Hp.
Timp.
Perc.
Solo Perc.
(Mar.)
mf
mp
p
pp
Vn. I
Vn. II
unis.
pp
Va.
unis.
pp
Vc.
div.
pp
Cb.
p

Picc.
Fl. 1 2
Ob. 1 2 3
Cl. 1 2 3
Bsn. 1 2 3
Hn. 1 3 5 2 4 6
Tpt. 1 2 3
Tbn. 1 2
3 Tuba
Hp.
Timp.
Perc. 1 2 3
Solo Perc.
MY
pppp
mf
pppp
8va
Vn. I
Vn. II
Va.
Vc.
Cb.

34
Picc.
Fl. 1 2
Ob. 1 2 3
Cl. 1 2 3
Bsn. 1 2 3
Hn. 1 3 5 2 4 6
Tpt. 1 2 3
Tbn. 1 2 3
Tuba
Hp.
Timp.
Perc. 1 2 3
Solo Perc.
pppp
mf
pppp
Vn. I
Vn. II
Va.
Vc.
Cb.

35
Picc.
Fl.
Ob.
solo
Cl.
Bsn.
Hn.
Tpt.
Tbn.
Tuba
Hp.
Timp.
Perc.
Solo Perc.
Vn. I
Vn. II
Va.
Vc.
Cb.
unis.
gliss.

Picc.
Fl.
Ob.
Cl.
Bsn.
Hn.
Tpt.
Tbn.
Tuba
Hp.
Timp.
Perc.
Solo Perc.
Vn. I
Vn. II
Va.
Vc.
Cb.

accelerando poco a poco al
Picc.
Fl.
Ob.
Cl.
Bsn.
(non dim.)
Hn.
non dim.
Tpt.
Tbn.
Tuba
Hp.
Timp.
Perc.
Solo Perc.
non dim.
accelerando poco a poco al
Vn. I
Vn. II
Va.
Vc.
Cb.
div.

36
♩ = 76
a tempo (♩ = 58)
Picc.
Fl.
Ob.
Cl.
Bsn.
Hn.
Tpt.
Tbn.
Tuba
Hp.
Timp.
Perc.
Solo Perc.
Vn. I
Vn. II
Va.
Vc.
Cb.
a2

senza misura (𝅗𝅥 = 58)
Picc.
Fl.
Ob.
Cl.
Bsn.
Hn.
Tpt.
Tbn.
Tuba
Hp.
Cb B♮
l. v.
Timp.
Perc.
Antique Cymbal
HP
Solo Perc.
MY
pesante
senza misura (𝅗𝅥 = 58)
Vn. I
Vn. II
Va.
Vc.
Cb.

* precise coordination of these instruments' parts is unnecessary at this point

Picc.
Fl.
Ob.
Cl.
Bsn.
Hn.
Tpt.
Tbn.
Tuba
Hp.
Timp.
Perc.
Solo Perc.
Vn. I
Vn. II
Va.
Vc.
Cb.
gliss.

Ob.
Cl.
Bsn.
Hn.
Tpt.
Tbn.
Tuba
Hp.
l. v.
F♮
C♯
A♮
E♭
F♯
Timp.
Perc.
Solo Perc.
Vn. I
Vn. II
Va.
Vc.
Cb.

Picc.
Fl. 1 2
Ob. 1 2 3
Cl. 1 2 3
Bsn. 1 2 3
Hn. 1 3 5 2 4 6
Tpt. 1 2 3
Tbn. 1 2
3 Tuba
Hp.
Timp.
Perc. 1 2 3
Solo Perc.
SY
pppp
mf
pp
f
p
f
rit.
p
pp
Vn. I
Vn. II
unis.
Va.
p
gliss.
Vc.
gliss.
Cb.

37
a tempo (♩ = 58)
Picc.
Fl.
Ob.
Cl.
Bsn.
Hn.
Tpt.
Tbn.
Tuba
Hp.
Timp.
Perc.
Solo Perc.
Vn. I
Vn. II
Va.
Vc.
Cb.
con sord.
2. con sord.
4. con sord.
a2
gliss.
MF
Tam-Tam
l.v.
a tempo (♩ = 58)
unis.

Picc.
Fl.
Ob.
Cl.
Bsn.
Hn.
Tpt.
Tbn.
Tuba
Hp.
l. v.
C♮ E♮
B♮
E♭ A♭ G♮
F♮
D♭
Timp.
Perc.
Solo Perc.
ossia:
Vn. I
Vn. II
6 soli
(gli altri tacet)
Va.
Vc.
Cb.
gliss.

Picc.
Fl. 1 2
(2.)
Ob. 1 2 3
Cl. 1 2 3
1. solo
Bsn. 1 2 3
Hn. 1 3 5 2 4 6
Tpt. 1 2 3
Tbn. 1 2 3
Tuba
Hp.
Timp.
Perc. 1 2 3
Solo Perc.
non cresc.
Vn. I
Vn. II
tutti, unis.
Va.
Vc.
Cb.

38
Picc.
Fl. 1 2
Ob. 1 2
Ob. 3
Cl. 1 2
Cl. 3
Bsn. 1 2
Bsn. 3
Hn. 1 3
Hn. 5 2
Hn. 4 6
Tpt. 1 2
Tpt. 3
Tbn. 1 2
Tbn. 3 Tuba
Hp.
Timp.
Perc. 1
Perc. 2
Perc. 3
Solo Perc.
Vn. I
pppp
pp
Vn. II
pp
Va.
Vc.
Cb.

Picc.
Fl. 1 2
Ob. 1 2 3
Cl. 1 2 3
Bsn. 1 2 3
Hn. 1 3 5 2 4 6
Tpt. 1 2 3
Tbn. 1 2
3 Tuba
Hp.
l. v.
mf
l. v.
Timp.
Perc. 1 2 3
Solo Perc.
steel drum sticks
Steel Drum(s)
note: avoid playing tremolo on this instrument unless specifically indicated
mfs
pp
mfs
pp
Vn. I
Vn. II
Va.
Vc.
Cb.
unis. pizz.
mp
mp

senza misura (♩ = ca. 58)
Picc.
Fl. 1 2
Ob. 1 2 3
Cl. 1 2 3
Bsn. 1 2 3
Hn. 1 3 5 2 4 6
Tpt. 1 2 3
Tbn. 1 2
3 Tuba
Hp.
Timp.
Perc. 1 2 3
Solo Perc.
ppp < p
mf
p
senza misura (♩ = ca. 58)
Vn. I
Vn. II
Va.
tutti, div.
pp
div.
Vc.
tutti, unis.
pp
div.
Cb.
arco
pp

39
a tempo (♩ = 58)
Picc.
Fl.
Ob.
Cl.
Bsn.
Hn.
2.
senza sord.
6.
Tpt.
Tbn.
Tuba
Hp.
Timp.
Perc.
accel. → a tempo → rit. molto → ♩ = 40 a tempo rit. → al ♩ = 40
Solo Perc.
a tempo (♩ = 58)
Vn. I
Vn. II
Va.
Vc.
Cb.

Fl.
Ob.
Cl.
Bsn.
senza sord.
senza sord.
Hn.
Tpt.
Tbn.
Tuba
Timp.
Perc.
Solo Perc.
Vn. I
Vn. II
Va.
Vc.
Cb.

Fl.
Ob.
Cl.
Bsn.
Hn.
Tpt.
Tbn.
Tuba
Timp.
Perc.
Solo Perc.
Vn. I
Vn. II
Va.
Vc.
Cb.
a2
senza sord.
gliss.

Picc.
Fl. 1 2
Ob. 1 2 3
Cl. 1 2 3
Bsn. 1 2 3
Hn. 1 3 5 2 4 6
Tpt. 1 2 3
Tbn. 1 2
3 Tuba
Hp.
Timp.
Perc. 1 2 3
Solo Perc.
Vn. I
Vn. II
Va.
Vc.
Cb.
(a2)
a2
2.
C♯ → C
B → B♭
—MF
Suspended Cymbal
—SY
Tam-Tam
Bass Drum
non. div.
unis.
div.

* if practicable, this drum set should be a complete and self-contained entity separated from the other solo instruments.

Picc.
Fl.
Ob.
Cl.
Bsn.
a2
a2
Hn.
Tpt.
2.
a2
Tbn.
Tuba
Hp.
Timp.
Perc.
Solo Perc.
Suspended Cymbals
1.
2.
ff
Chinese Cymbal
Vn. I
Vn. II
Va.
Vc.
arco
pizz.
Cb.
arco
pizz.

Picc.
Fl.
Ob.
Cl.
Bsn.
Hn.
Tpt.
Tbn.
Tuba
Hp.
Timp.
Perc.
Solo Perc.
Vn. I
Vn. II
Va.
Vc.
Cb.
a2
(Suspended Cymbal)
HY
l. v.
(Bass Drum)
solo
div.
arco
pizz.
(non div.)

41
Picc.
Fl.
Ob.
Cl.
Bsn.
a2
Hn.
a2
a2
Tpt.
Tbn.
(a2)
Tuba
Hp.
Timp.
Cowbell
SD butt
ff
Tambourine with knuckles
ff
Perc.
f
ff
Solo Perc.
unis.
Vn. I
unis.
Vn. II
unis.
Va.
Vc.
Cb.

Picc.
Fl.
Ob.
Cl.
Bsn.
Hn.
Tpt.
Tbn.
Tuba
Hp.
Timp.
Perc.
Solo Perc.
with stick (damp hi-hat with fingers)
Vn. I
Vn. II
Va.
Vc.
Cb.

Picc.
Fl.
Ob.
Cl.
Bsn.
Hn.
Tpt.
Tbn.
Tuba
Hp.
Timp.
solo
HF
Perc.
Solo Perc.
Vn. I
div.a3
Vn. II
div.a3
Va.
Vc.
Cb.

Picc.
Fl. 1 2
Ob. 1 2
3
Cl. 1 2
3
Bsn. 1 2
3
(a2)
Hn. 1 3
5 2
4 6
a2
(a2)
Tpt. 1 2
3
Tbn. 1 2
3 Tuba
a2
Hp.
Timp.
ff
Perc. 1
2
3
ff
mf
Solo Perc.
with foot pedal
Vn. I
unis.
Vn. II
unis.
Va.
Vc.
Cb.

42
Picc.
Fl. 1 2
Ob. 1 2
3
Cl. 1 2
3
Bsn. 1 2
3
Hn. 1 3
5 2
4 6
Tpt. 1 2
3
Tbn. 1 2
3 Tuba
Hp.
B♯ G♯ E♮ D♮ A♮ C♯
Timp.
Suspended Cymbal
(—SD butt)
Perc. 1 2 3
Solo Perc.
Vn. I
Vn. II
(non div.)
Va.
Vc.
Cb.

Picc.
Fl. 1 2
Ob. 1 2 3
Cl. 1 2 3
Bsn. 1 2 3
Hn. 1 3 5 2 4 6
Tpt. 1 2 3
Tbn. 1 2
3 Tuba
Hp.
G♮ D♯ A♯ F♯
B♮
Timp.
Perc. 1 2 3
Solo Perc.
SD
near domes
normale
mp
Vn. I
Vn. II
(non div.)
Va.
Vc.
Cb.

Picc.
Fl. 1 2
Ob. 1 2 3
Cl. 1 2 3
Bsn. 1 2 3
(2.)
(1.)
a2
2.
1.
Hn. 1 3 5 2 4 6
Tpt. 1 2 3
Tbn. 1 2 3
Tuba
Hp.
C♮ A♭
E♭ G♭ D♮
C♯ A♮ F♮
G♯
C♮
Timp.
Perc. 1 2 3
Solo Perc.
poco f
mp
poco f
mp
Vn. I
Vn. II
Va.
Vc.
Cb.

43
Picc.
Fl. 1 2
Ob. 1 2 3
Cl. 1 2 3
Bsn. 1 2 3
(2.)
(1.)
dim.
Hn. 1 3 5 2 4 6
6.
Tpt. 1 2 3
Tbn. 1 2
Tuba 3
Hp.
G♮
F#
Cb Eb F♮ Ab
gliss.
l. v.
Timp.
Perc. 1 2 3
Solo Perc.
SD butt
with stick
come sopra
Vn. I
Vn. II
Va.
Vc.
Cb.

Picc. 1
Fl. 1 2
Ob. 1 2
Ob. 3
Cl. 1 2
Cl. 3
Bsn. 1 2
Bsn. 3
Hn. 1 3
Hn. 5 2
Hn. 4 6
Tpt. 1 2
Tpt. 3
Tbn. 1 2
Tbn. 3 Tuba
Hp.
Timp.
Perc. 1 2 3
Solo Perc.
Vn. I
Vn. II
Va.
Vc.
Cb.
div. a2
div. a4
a2

Picc.
8va
Fl. 1 2
Ob. 1 2
3
Cl. 1
2
3
Bsn. 1 2
3
ff
a2
Hn. 1 3
5 2
4 6
Tpt. 1 2
3
Tbn. 1 2
3 Tuba
Hp.
Timp.
HF solo
(Cowbell)
SD butt
Suspended Cymbal
l. v.
Perc. 1
2
3
(Tambourine)
(with knuckles)
(Bass Drum)
solo
fff
ffff
Solo Perc.
cymbals normale
with foot pedal
Vn. I
unis.
div.
a4
Vn. II
non div.
Va.
div.
Vc.
Cb.

44
Picc.
8va
Fl. 1 2
a2
Ob. 1 2
3
Cl. 1
2
3
Bsn. 1 2
3
Hn. 1 3
5 2
4 6
Tpt. 1 2
3
Tbn. 1 2
3 Tuba
Hp.
Timp.
Perc. 1
2
3
p
pppp
Solo Perc.
l.v.
to Timbales
Vn. I
Vn. II
Va.
Vc.
Cb.
div.
mf

Picc.
Fl. 1 2
Ob. 1 2 3
Cl. 1 2 3
Bsn. 1 2 3
Hn. 1 3 5 2 4 6
p ppp
Tpt. 1 2 3
Tbn. 1 2 3
Tuba
Hp.
Timp.
Perc. 1 2 3
Solo Perc.
Vn. I
Vn. II
Va.
Vc.
Cb.

Picc.
Fl.
Ob.
Cl.
Bsn.
Hn.
Tpt.
Tbn.
Tuba
Hp.
Timp.
Perc.
Solo Perc.
Vn. I
Vn. II
Va.
Vc.
Cb.
poco f
poco f
—MF
poco f

Picc.
Fl. 1 2
Ob. 1 2 3
Cl. 1 2 3
Bsn. 1 2 3
Hn. 1 3 5 2 4 6
Tpt. 1 2 3
Tbn. 1 2 3
Tuba
Hp.
Timp.
Perc. 1 2 3
Chimes
let all notes ring
Solo Perc.
Vn. I
Vn. II
Va.
Vc.
Cb.
pppp
a2
ff
2.
3.

45
Picc.
Fl.
Ob.
Cl.
Bsn.
Hn.
Tpt.
Tbn.
Tuba
Hp.
Timp.
Perc.
Solo Perc.
Timbales
SD
Bongos
Vn. I
Vn. II
Va.
Vc.
Cb.
a2

Picc.
Fl.
Ob.
Cl.
Bsn.
Hn.
Tpt.
Tbn.
Tuba
Hp.
Timp.
C→D
D→C
Perc.
Antique Cymbals
Solo Perc.
Snare Drum
Vn. I
Vn. II
Va.
Vc.
Cb.

(*) a real blacksmith's anvil, not the "modern" orchestral substitute

Picc.
Fl. 1 2
Ob. 1 2 3
Cl. 1 2 3
Bsn. 1 2 3
Hn. 1 3 5 2 4 6
Tpt. 1 2 3
Tbn. 1 2 3
Tuba
Hp.
Timp.
Perc. 1 2 3
Solo Perc.
Vn. I
Vn. II
Va.
Vc.
Cb.

47
Picc.
Fl. 1 2
Ob. 1 2
3
Cl. 1 2
3
Bsn. 1 2
3
Hn. 1 3
5 2
4 6
Tpt. 1 2
3
Tbn. 1 2
Tuba 3
Hp.
Timp.
Perc. 1
2
3
Solo Perc.
Tom-toms
SD
cresc.
Vn. I
Vn. II
Va.
Vc.
Cb.

Picc.
Fl. 1 2
Ob. 1 2 3
Cl. 1 2 3
Bsn. 1 2 3
Hn. 1 3 5 2 4 6
Tpt. 1 2 3
Tbn. 1 2 3
Tuba
2.
Tuba
Hp.
Timp.
Perc. 1 2 3
Solo Perc.
cresc.
Vn. I
Vn. II
Va.
Vc.
Cb.
non dim.
div.

Picc.
Fl. 1 2
Ob. 1 2 3
Cl. 1 2 3
1. Solo
Bsn. 1 2 3
Hn. 1 3 5 2 4 6
Tpt. 1 2 3
Tbn. 1 2 3
Tuba
Hp.
Timp.
Perc. 1 2 3
(Snare Drum)
Solo Perc.
Vn. I
Vn. II
Va.
Vc.
Cb.
unis.

48
Picc.
Fl.
Ob.
Cl.
Bsn.
Hn.
Tpt.
Tbn.
Tuba
Hp.
Timp.
Perc.
Solo Perc.
Vn. I
Vn. II
Va.
Vc.
Cb.
più p
a2
fast arpeggio
l.v.
E♮ A♮
Xylophone
LP

Picc.
Fl. 1 2
Ob. 1 2
3
Cl. 1 2
3
Bsn. 1 2
ppp
3
ppp
Hn. 1 3
5 2
4 6
Tpt. 1 2
3
Tbn. 1 2
3 Tuba
Hp.
Timp.
Perc. 1
(Xyl.)
2
3
Solo Perc.
Vn. I
Vn. II
Va.
Vc.
Cb.

49
Picc.
Fl.
Ob.
Cl.
Bsn.
Hn.
Tpt.
Tbn.
Tuba
Hp.
Timp.
Perc.
Solo Perc.
Vn. I
Vn. II
Va.
Vc.
Cb.
solo
con sord.
(Xyl.)
Castanets
Log Drums
SR
B♭
C♮

Picc.
Fl. 1 2
Ob. 1 2 3
Cl. 1 2 3
Bsn. 1 2 3
Hn. 1 3 5 2 4 6
Tpt. 1 2 3
Tbn. 1 2 3
Tuba
Hp.
G♭
B♮
G♮ C♯
D♯
F♯ C♮
D♮
Timp.
Perc. 1 2 3
Solo Perc.
Vn. I
Vn. II
Va.
Vc.
Cb.

Picc.
Fl.
Ob.
solo
mp
Cl.
1.
Bsn.
Hn.
Tpt.
Tbn.
Tuba
Hp.
F♮
B♭
C♯
G♯
f
mf
Timp.
Perc.
Solo Perc.
Vn. I
Vn. II
Va.
Vc.
Cb.

Picc.
Fl. 1 2
Ob. 1 2
3
Cl. 1 2
3
Bsn. 1 2
1.
3
Hn. 1 3
5 2
4 6
non cresc.
non cresc.
non cresc.
Tpt. 1 2
3
Tbn. 1 2
3 Tuba
Hp.
F♯
non dim.
l.v.
Timp.
Perc. 1
2
3
Xylophone
LP
Solo Perc.
(Log Drum 4)
Vn. I
Vn. II
Va.
Vc.
Cb.
div.a3
gliss.
8va
non cresc.

50
Picc.
Fl.
Ob.
Cl.
Bsn.
Hn.
Tpt.
Tbn.
Tuba
Hp.
Timp.
Perc.
(Castanets)
Wood Blocks
MR
(Log Drums)
Solo Perc.
unis.
Vn. I
Vn. II
Va.
Vc.
Cb.

Picc.
Fl. 1 2
Ob. 1 2 3
Cl. 1 2 3
Bsn. 1 2 3
Hn. 1 3 5 2 4 6
Tpt. 1 2 3
Tbn. 1 2 3
Tuba
Hp.
Timp.
Perc. 1 2 3
mf
ppp
Solo Perc.
Vn. I
Vn. II
Va.
Vc.
Cb.

Picc.
Fl. 1 2
Ob. 1 2 3
Cl. 1 2 3
Bsn. 1 2 3
Hn. 1 3 5 2 4 6
Tpt. 1 2 3
Tbn. 1 2 3
Tuba
Hp.
Timp.
Perc. 1 2 3
mf
Solo Perc.
Vn. I
Vn. II
Va.
Vc.
Cb.

51
Picc.
Fl. 1 2
Ob. 1 2
3
Cl. 1 2
3
Bsn. 1 2
3
Hn. 1 3
5 2
4 6
2. senza sord.
a2 senza sord.
Tpt. 1 2
3
Tbn. 1 2
3 Tuba
Tuba
Hp.
Timp.
MF
Perc. 1
2
3
Solo Perc.
Bass Drum
Vn. I
Vn. II
Va.
Vc.
Cb.

Picc.
Fl.
Ob.
Cl.
Bsn.
Hn.
Tpt.
Tbn.
Tuba
Hp.
Timp.
Perc.
Solo Perc.
Vn. I
Vn. II
Va.
Vc.
Cb.
(2.)
(a2)
(Tuba)
Tamtam
l.v.
B. Dr.

52
Picc.
Fl.
Ob.
Cl.
Bsn.
(1.)
Hn.
(2.)
(a2)
Tpt.
Tbn.
Tuba
a2
Hp.
Timp.
Perc.
l.v.
Solo Perc.
Wood Blocks
Log Drums
Bass Drum
Bongos
Timbales
Vn. I
Vn. II
Va.
Vc.
Cb.

Picc.
Fl.
Ob.
Cl.
Bsn.
Hn.
Tpt.
Tbn.
Tuba
Hp.
Timp.
Perc.
Solo Perc.
Vn. I
Vn. II
Va.
Vc.
Cb.
l.v.

Picc.
Fl. 1 2
a2
Ob. 1 2 3
Cl. 1 2 3
Bsn. 1 2 3
(2.)
Hn. 1 3 5 2 4 6
(a2)
senza sord.
a2, senza sord.
Tpt. 1 2 3
2.
Tbn. 1 2
Tbn. 3
Tuba
Hp.
Timp.
Perc. 1 2 3
l.v.
Solo Perc.
Vn. I
Vn. II
Va.
Vc.
Cb.

53
Picc.
(a2)
Fl.
Ob.
Cl.
Bsn.
Hn.
Tpt.
Tbn.
Tuba
Hp.
Timp.
Anvil
l.v.
Perc.
Solo
Perc.
Vn. I
Vn. II
Va.
Vc.
Cb.

Picc.
Fl. 1 2
(a2)
Ob. 1 2 3
Cl. 1 2 3
Bsn. 1 2 3
Hn. 1 3 5 2 4 6
Tpt. 1 2 3
Tbn. 1 2
3 Tuba
Hp.
Timp.
Perc. 1 2 3
Solo Perc.
Vn. I
Vn. II
Va.
Vc.
Cb.

Picc.
Fl.
Ob.
Cl.
Bsn.
Hn.
Tpt.
Tbn.
Tuba
Hp.
Timp.
Perc.
Solo Perc.
Vn. I
Vn. II
Va.
Vc.
Cb.
(a2)

* If bass trombone lacks the low B♮, omit it (i.e., do not play one octave higher).
** If thunder sheet is insufficiently loud or realistic in color, the sheet should be amplified or the sound electronically synthesized.

Picc.
Fl. 1 2
Ob. 1 2
3
Cl. 1 2
3
Bsn. 1 2
3
(a2)
Hn. 1 3
(a2)
5 2
(a2)
4 6
Tpt. 1 2
3
1.
Tbn. 1 2
(a2)
3 Tuba
Hp.
—HF
solo
Timp.
fff
Perc. 1
2
3
f
mf
p
mf
p
ppp
Solo Perc.
Vn. I
Vn. II
Va.
Vc.
Cb.

Picc.
Fl.
a2
(a2)
Ob.
Cl.
Bsn.
Hn.
Tpt.
Tbn.
Tuba
Hp.
Timp.
Perc.
Tamtam
secco
Solo Perc.
Vn. I
Vn. II
Va.
Vc.
Cb.

Picc.
Fl. 1 2
8va
Ob. 1 2 3
Cl. 1 2 3
Bsn. 1 2 3
Hn. 1 3 5 2 4 6
a2
Tpt. 1 2 3
Tbn. 1 2
Tbn. 3
3 Tuba
Hp.
Timp.
Perc. 1 2 3
Solo Perc.
unis.
Vn. I
div.
Vn. II
div.
Va.
Vc.
div.
Cb.

Contrabasses without extensions should tune their E strings to E♭.

Picc.
Fl. 1 2
Ob. 1 2 3
Cl. 1 2 3
Bsn. 1 2 3
Hn. 1 3 5 2 4 6
Tpt. 1 2 3
Tbn. 1 2 3
Tuba
Hp.
Timp.
Perc. 1 2 3
Solo Perc.
Vn. I
Vn. II
Va.
Vc.
Cb.

56
♪ = ♪ (sempre)
Picc.
Fl.
Ob.
Cl.
Bsn.
Hn.
Tpt.
Tbn.
Tuba
Hp.
Timp.
HF
fff
Perc.
Solo Perc.
♪ = ♪ (sempre)
Vn. I
Vn. II
Va.
Vc.
Cb.

Picc.
Fl. 1 2
Ob. 1 2 3
Cl. 1 2 3
Bsn. 1 2 3
Hn. 1 3 5 2 4 6
Tpt. 1 2 3
Tbn. 1 2 3
Tuba
Hp.
Timp.
Perc. 1 2 3
Solo Perc.
Vn. I
Vn. II
Va.
Vc.
Cb.

Picc.
Fl.
Ob.
Cl.
Bsn.
Hn.
Tpt.
Tbn.
Tuba
Hp.
Timp.
Perc.
Solo Perc.
Vn. I
Vn. II
Va.
Vc.
Cb.

57
Picc.
Fl.
Ob.
Cl.
Bsn.
Hn.
Tpt.
Tbn.
Tuba
Hp.
Timp.
Perc.
(Bass Drum)
ff
Solo Perc.
Vn. I
Vn. II
Va.
Vc.
Cb.

Picc.
Fl. 1 2
Ob. 1 2 3
Cl. 1 2 3
Bsn. 1 2 3
Hn. 1 3 5 2 4 6
Tpt. 1 2 3
Tbn. 1 2 3
Tuba
Hp.
Timp.
Perc. 1 2 3
Solo Perc.
Vn. I
Vn. II
Va.
Vc.
Cb.

Picc.
Fl. 1 2
Ob. 1 2 3
Cl. 1 2 3
Bsn. 1 2 3
Hn. 1 3 5 2 4 6
Tpt. 1 2 3
Tbn. 1 2 3
Tuba
Hp.
Timp.
Perc. 1 2 3
Solo Perc.
Vn. I
Vn. II
Va.
Vc.
Cb.

58
accel. impercettibile e graduale al 60
Picc.
Fl. 1 2
Ob. 1 2 3
Cl. 1 2 3
Bsn. 1 2 3
Hn. 1 3 5 2 4 6
Tpt. 1 2 3
Tbn. 1 2 3
Tuba
Hp.
Timp.
Perc. 1 2 3
Solo Perc.
Bass Drum
accel. impercettibile e graduale al 60
Vn. I
Vn. II
Va.
Vc.
Cb.

Picc.
Fl.
Ob.
Cl.
Bsn.
Hn.
Tpt.
Tbn.
Tuba
Hp.
Timp.
Perc.
HF
Tom-toms
4. 3. 2.
Solo Perc.
Bongo 1
Timbales
2. 1.
Bongo 2
Vn. I
Vn. II
Va.
Vc.
Cb.

Picc.
Fl.
Ob.
Cl.
Bsn.
Hn.
Tpt.
Tbn.
Tuba
Hp.
Timp.
Perc.
Solo
Perc.
Vn. I
Vn. II
Va.
Vc.
Cb.

Picc.
Fl. 1 2
Ob. 1 2 3
Cl. 1 2 3
Bsn. 1 2 3
Hn. 1 3 5 2 4 6
Tpt. 1 2 3
Tbn. 1 2 3
Tuba
Hp.
Timp.
Perc. 1 2 3
Solo Perc.
Vn. I
Vn. II
Va.
Vc.
Cb.
f
p
f
p
f
p

59
Picc.
Fl. 1 2
Ob. 1 2 3
Cl. 1 2 3
Bsn. 1 2 3
Hn. 1 3 5 2 4 6
Tpt. 1 2 3
Tbn. 1 2 3
Tuba
Hp.
Timp.
Perc. 1 2 3
Solo Perc.
Vn. I
Vn. II
Va.
Vc.
Cb.

Picc.
Fl. 1 2
Ob. 1 2 3
Cl. 1 2 3
Bsn. 1 2 3
Hn. 1 3 5 2 4 6
Tpt. 1 2 3
Tbn. 1 2 3
Tuba
Hp.
Timp.
Perc. 1 2 3
Solo Perc.
Vn. I
Vn. II
Va.
Vc.
Cb.

60
𝅗𝅥. = 96
Picc.
Fl. 1 2
Ob. 1 2 3
Cl. 1 2 3
Bsn. 1 2 3
Hn. 1 3 5 2 4 6
Tpt. 1 2 3
Tbn. 1 2
3 Tuba
Hp.
Timp.
Perc. 1 2 3
Solo Perc.
𝅗𝅥. = 96
Vn. I
Vn. II
Va.
Vc.
Cb.

Picc.
Fl. 1 2
Ob. 1 2 3
Cl. 1 2 3
Bsn. 1 2 3
Hn. 1 3 5 2 4 6
Tpt. 1 2 3
Tbn. 1 2 3
Tuba
Hp.
Timp.
Perc. 1 2 3
Solo Perc.
Vn. I
Vn. II
Va.
Vc.
Cb.

61
Picc.
Fl. 1 2
Ob. 1 2
Ob. 3
Cl. 1 2
Cl. 3
Bsn. 1 2
Bsn. 3
Hn. 1 3
Hn. 5 2
Hn. 4 6
Tpt. 1 2
Tpt. 3
Tbn. 1 2
Tbn. 3 Tuba
Hp.
Timp.
Perc. 1
Perc. 2
Perc. 3
Solo Perc.
Vn. I
Vn. II
Va.
Vc.
Cb.
ftz.
a2
solo
Large rachet
Snare Drum
Suspended Cymbal
SY
(Bongo 1)
(Timbales)
(Bass Drum)
div.
unis.
(div.)

Picc.
Fl. 1 2
Ob. 1 2 3
Cl. 1 2 3
Bsn. 1 2 3
a2
(a2)
Hn. 1 3 5 2 4 6
Tpt. 1 2 3
Tbn. 1 2 3 Tuba
3.
Hp.
Timp.
Perc. 1 2 3
Tam-Tam
l. v.
fff
pp
ff
Tom-toms
Solo Perc.
Vn. I
unis.
gliss.
Vn. II
Va.
Vc.
div.
Cb.

Picc.
Fl.
Ob.
Cl.
Bsn.
Hn.
Tpt.
Tbn.
Tuba
Hp.
Timp.
Anvil
Perc.
Solo Perc.
Vn. I
Vn. II
Va.
Vc.
Cb.

* these words are meant to reinforce the guiro gesture's meaning, not to be articulated verbally.

Deo Gratias
June 7, 1997